LIVING IN GOSHEN

Pharaoh's Lament

Elijah Centre
Project
Heritage

Pharaoh's Lament

Based on the "Living in Goshen" Series
Created by Elijah Centre Project Heritage

Orginally printed in Trinidad & Tobago
First Printing 2020

ISBN 978-976-43-0020-5

Congress
PublishingHouse

Dedicated to the Children of Congress WBN

Keep Goshen in your hearts!

Pharaoh's Song

How dare Moses!
He's such a pest!
Speaking to me like he knows best!

I've ruled Egypt for a long time
And I know how to protect what's mine.

Turning my waters into blood!
Sending frogs and flies in floods.
Killing my horses, sheep and cows!
To Moses's God I will never bow.

This is my Egypt!
This is my land!

And I rule everything by my hand.

Moses and his slaves will have to see -
there is no power greater than me!

Pharaoh's Lament

I was the great ruler of Egypt,
nations looked up to me.
My country was quite wealthy,
and rich with power you see.

From the tall and mighty buildings,
to the systems of trade –
Egypt was very prosperous,
our strength would never fade.

I, the Great and Mighty Pharaoh,
took pride in my state.
Until the day that man called Moses,
foretold of my ill fate.
He brought a Divine message –
but I did not even care.
Four strong yet simple words,
I did not want to hear.

I did not want to listen,
I did not want to know.
But he kept commanding –

'Let my people go!'

So I grew proud and decided,
to show him my great power.
I chose to harden my heart,
with each passing hour.

But things just got worse,
no magician could aid!
So my land was destroyed,
plague after plague...

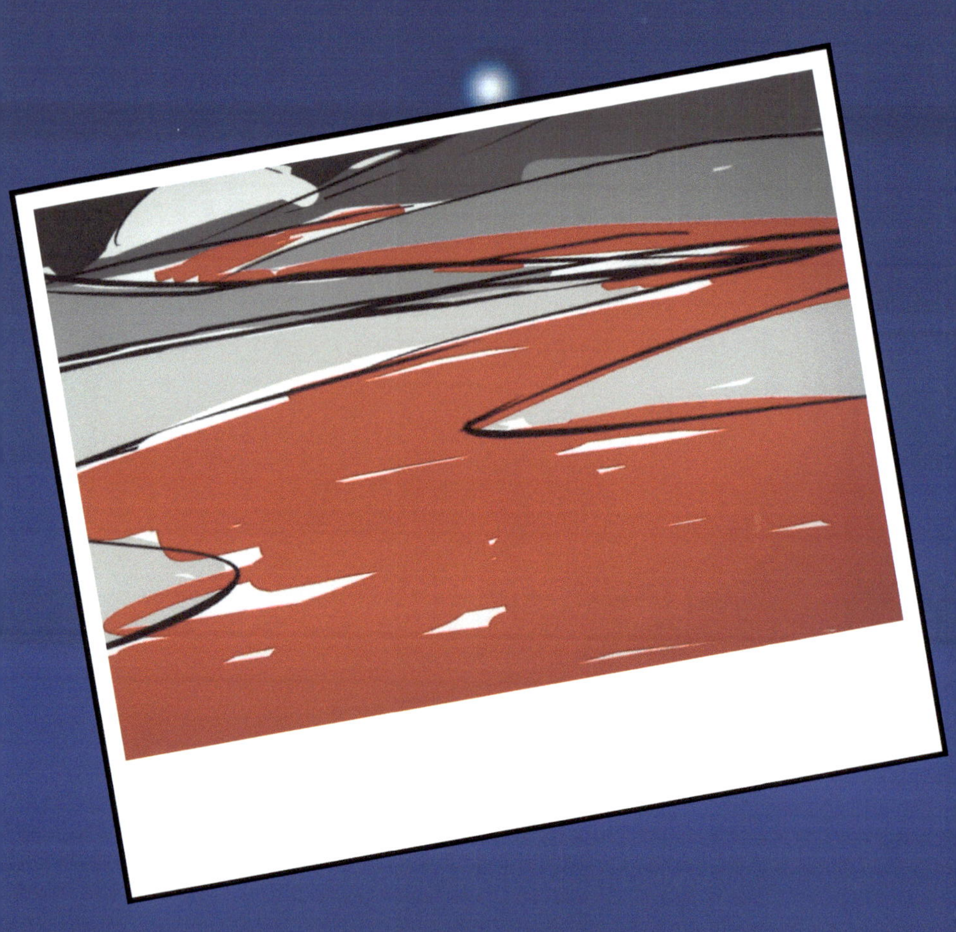

First Moses turned the waters
into blood you see.
But so did my magicians -
easy as 1-2-3!

Then came the leaping frogs
that leapt everywhere,
But my magician's magic
also made frogs appear.

Then came the crawling lice,
but things got quite odd:
The magic did not work
for it was the finger of God!

This was followed by flies,
it was no small amount.
So many swarmed over us,
you could not even count!

But what happened next,
sent my land into shock!
The fifth plague was released,
and killed all our livestock!

The days just grew harder,
full of trouble and toil.
Next, my people were struck
with festering boils!

Still I did not bow,
my pride did not fail.
So my people were struck
with the plague of hail.

I begged Moses for help,
but to him I was unjust.
So his God tormented Egypt,
with a plague of locusts.

When the plague of darkness came,
I was out of my mind.
I could not see for three days,
I thought I was blind!

This last plague I'll remember,
throughout all time.
It has touched the very core
of all that is mine.

Oh, my people!
What am I to do?

All my strength and magic,
have not protected you.

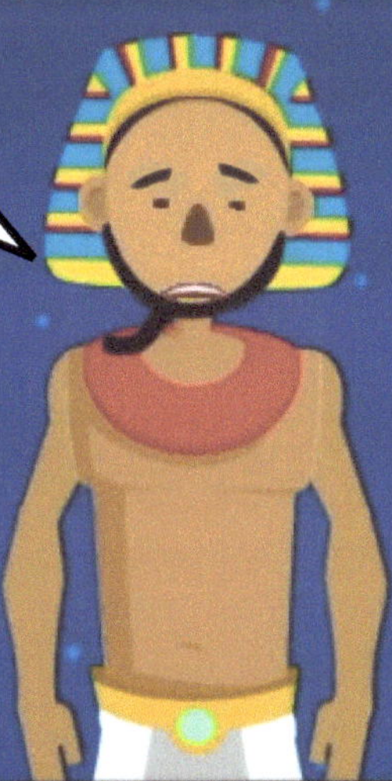

I have to admit -
I think Moses has won.
This night his God has killed
Egypt's firstborn sons.

So I sit here, tired and weary you know.
I think it's time to giveup and

Let God's people go!

"Living in Goshen" was produced by Elijah Centre Project Heritage.

Elijah Centre is a unique, global, borderless, Kingdom community, founded on biblical principles and recognizing Jesus Christ as its head. With its primary base in Trinidad & Tobago, called the Nexus, Elijah Centre has locations in cities around the globe, referred to as Embassies. For more information, visit:

www.elijahcentre.org

Project Heritage is the People Group ministry within Elijah Centre for children up to age 11. Project Heritage focuses on holistic development based on the pattern of maturity demonstrated by Jesus throughout his childhood. For more information, visit:

www.projectheritage.org

Elijah Centre is the Creative Core of Congress WBN, a global, faith-based organization affecting human, social and national transformation throughout the earth. For more information, visit:

www.congresswbn.org